Seasick Blue

Poems from the Tower Poetry Summer School 2008

Edited by Jane Draycott and Frances Leviston

Published by Tower Poetry, Christ Church, Oxford, 2009
Designed by Jamie Shaw (design@jamietshaw.co.uk)
Illustrations by Rachel Yates

p.5: JBS 21, Tuscan School, (c.1440–50), Scenes from the Life of St.
Benedict, Abba Macarius & Others—reproduced by permission of the
Governing Body of Christ Church, Oxford

ISBN 978-0-9549932-4-5
Printed in the United Kingdom by Hunts

Contents

Preface v

Introduction vii

Ailie MacDonald
Conjoined 2
America 3
Gorkie Cratur 4

John Clegg
Scenes from the Life of St Benedict 6
The Sting 7
Portrait of Lee Marvin As America 9

Colette Sensier
Graduation Wearing Salmon 12
Riddle 14
La Vanille Crocodile Farm, Mauritius 16

Richard O'Brien
The Day the Revolution Came 18
Honey in the Bible 21
Dry Land 22

Charlotte Geater
Lost in Broadcast 24
Soft 25
Boil 26

Rees Arnott-Davies
Amalfi 28
Saint-Malo 29
The Turk 31

Annie Katchinska
Massachusetts 36
Panic Attack 37

Rowena Knight

Charon's Passengers   40

At Sea   41

Angel Beach   42

Emily Middleton

Breakfast with the Gods   44

Poppy Harvesting   46

The Faces   47

Antony Hurley

Exile   50

The Morning Garden   51

An August Evening with W.B.Yeats   52

The poets   **55**

Preface

Since 2000, Tower Poetry, which is based at Christ Church, Oxford, has developed a number of projects designed to encourage young adults in Britain to write and think about poetry. This booklet features the work of young poets who have taken part in two of Tower Poetry's core initiatives: the annual Christopher Tower Poetry Prize, now well-established as the UK's most prestigious poetry prize for 16–18 year-olds, and the Tower Poetry Summer School, a residential course which offers a group of poets between the ages of 18–23 years the chance to develop their writing and critical skills alongside top poets and creative writing tutors.

This is the fifth volume of poems emanating from the Tower Poetry Summer School held in Christ Church, Oxford, in August 2008.

Tower Poetry would like to thank the two tutors, Jane Draycott and Frances Leviston, for their hard work over the course of the week; and Professor David Morley who gave an evening reading of his poetry.

Introduction

The setting which Tower Poetry provides to the young
writers selected for its Summer School seems like a
charmed one: Christ Church's famous quadrangles
and gardens, the romance of the river meadows, the
Lewis Carroll tree, the remarkable dining-hall. All this,
combined with the extended opportunity to collaborate
in small groups creating new work, sparking off one
another, exploring together the one thing that interests
us all intensely: poetry. It's a generous scheme, and one
which Frances Leviston and I were very pleased to have
been invited to be part of in 2008. But the success of
the week depends even more vitally on the imaginative
and intellectual energy that the participants themselves
bring to it. As this anthology demonstrates, the young
writers we worked with were all, in their different visions
and approaches, fired with exactly the kind of drive to
break through to the poem-beyond-the poem which is
the mark of all memorable poetry. David Morley's guest
reading injected an inspiring sense of the possibilities
open to them as new voices, and it's a testimony to their
seriousness and hard work that several of the poets
represented here are already on their way to publication in
magazines and anthologies.

Jane Draycott and Frances Leviston

Ailie MacDonald

Conjoined

America

Gorkie Cratur

Conjoined

Your kin is an untiring youth, he skulks to the rhythm
Of the low-lying wind,
Beneath the desert and Neanderthal bones he often
Drops his shoulder to touch the stone.
A palm curves, he plants his broad hands and feet
over the land.
The dreary warning bells now ring
To draw us from our hill-top caves.
The ministers and lawmakers wait a little—
Burn a temple, build a barrier.
To cross back and forth, to move unerring through
Each stone-cast boundary.
Trade winds draw back from behind the barrier,
Its graffiti ink all smeared about on firstborns skin.
It is at once twinned and reversed, transcribed on the land:
Aramaic, blood-strong, undefeated king.

I would have held your hand, clutched onto coattails
Held cold-clawed onto our shared miracle—
The pink gut exposed
As he lights his phosphorous, begins to wait

It was all some miscalculation, some empty human fortitude
silently duplicated as the axle tips and slides
steep from the Western Bank
into a hot sea.
They dig into fields of wheat and maize;
While it grows, they wait—
And as the white light grapples above the arid land
We watch it fall from both sides of the barrier.

America

It was the summer, cold as the place drew close, and
hunkered to the land.
The worms were curling round each sod of green, and in
their weary gait
liked to think in the darkness how they knew of tar-hulled
ships
that sailed towards America —
of their pink brothers there, across the unbroken water, lying
hidden.

What the packed-in years of mud had pressed down to cast-iron
basalt rock
Sour milky eyes now stooped low to see — American breath
was flushed
And grew to stone
That they uncovered, they knew, was turning in the snow to
white and green
As the boats hit the cliffs, and wore across the bay.

Those timber houses our children knew
from days spent straying round each gunshot street of
Indiana, Monterey,
Soon clattered up to meet the earth in long slanting
canopies, and sceptres of steel.
If only those quiet men knew, what all those quiet worms
had known.

Shallow and sunlit, up from the soil we met:
To where great bow-backed mothers once had fed us all
From bowls of soylent-green and blue,
from under a great berth of stone.

Gorkie Cratur
Wind in Scottish Streets

Thaim that haena seen the figure o the wind
Come frae the north tae sing
On the gable-ends of hoose and kirk
Wudna ken his chuffie-cheekit face in the street;

Aw knorlie, his gut-pock dreeps laich
And lang owre the hairst nicht gloaming hour
His heid and nose follow our wurds in the mirk
An his een reach

Saft and soomin tae the wandering licht
Upon the warl's edge
as the herring-drave floister in bits upon the surface
coming thegither and breezin awa' again
in the solemn sunsingit reid o the sodium lamp
ye catch him gaun roon wi the smirry rain
and ken in a hunner year 'til aw be the same
the wind gaun roon wi the smirry rain.

Gorkie—disgusting   *Chuffie-cheekit*—fat faced
knorlie—knarly, covered in lumps   *gut-pock*—belly
laich—low   *hairst*—harvest   *soomin*—swimming/
floating   *herring-drave*—a shoal of herring
sunsingit—sunburnt

John Clegg

Scenes from the Life of St Benedict

The Sting

Portrait of Lee Marvin As America

Scenes From The Life Of St Benedict

(Christ Church Picture Gallery)

Inside a cloven hole in this rockwall
the day is night, the night is day to
Benedict, disputing with the skull
of Antonillus, noted idolater.

Macarius, his rival, squats bare-bummed
among a thornbush, preaching (even though
his psalter looks suspiciously unthumbed)
to what is either demon, pug or cow.

A gold-rigged camel nibbles on a cowslip
while Benedict, for some reason, looks on
from his tall cave split open like a hairlip.
The weather heaves with burned, stampeding oxen.

He teaches a hyena how to pray.
Monks in a harness lower bread and tallow.
He nails proclamations to the sky.
The devil plays a peasant like a cello.

The Sting

Paul Newman's still alive but only just;
it's not too early for an elegy
when death is all that's owed to anyone.
My sister, on the phone, complains how poetry
can play Scott Joplin ragtime on the words
but can't pinpoint the tragedy in loss:
we obviously don't go on forever
and he was old, well-loved and beautiful
till months ago, till lung cancer and chemo.
What can't be cured must be endured —
but poetry endures, and we're suspicious
of the single fact about the future
that we're put on earth with. Even so.

My sister says she's jettisoned her scheme
of heading for Chicago, city of icescraper
wind and deepdish pizza, setting for The Sting:
Paul Newman's masterpiece, my masterplan.
Among its grifters, conmen, card sharps,
gangsters, Feds and beautiful assassins
I lay the snare, I bait the hook and wire;
each poem is a scam artist or grifter
and Death is the eternal Mark or Sucker
in the very longest of long cons,
the schmuck who doesn't know he's being played.
We stall him, give him easy smiling answers
(this is called The Tale). Listen hard:

A Folsom convict starts his own religion
from his cell, calls it the Church Of New Song.
A mail-order thing. His one commandment
is the Prophet can't be put to death.
And he's the Prophet. And he's on Death Row.
He launches an appeal on these grounds;
while it winds its way to the Supreme Court,

he escapes. And then the warders notice
what his Church spelt out in acronym.
Convict, conman, con trick. Confidence. Poem.
Trick shuffle so 'Paul Newman's still alive'
and all the bunko squad turns up weeks later
is Greyhound stub, marked deck and funny money.

Portrait Of Lee Marvin As America

His face becomes a wilderness
of crag and scrubland: dynamited canyons
where the odd red wolf, the odd coyote wanders.

His insides turn to goldmines straining
on their pit-props, oil wells, the overdue
volcano under Yellowstone, a redwood's root-ball.

—

Buck naked on a barrel-raft, he drifts
along the Mississipi into Natchez.
Using a branch he snags his stovepipe hat from the rapids.

He whistles his theme tune. In the saloon,
nobody knows about his teeming democratic mass,
his hobo camps, his big rock candy mountain.

—

When he sleeps, they run a flag up his erection
and when he farts, Wall Street shudders
and when he smokes it's a forest fire.

He opens his mouth and a hundred convicts climb over.
He shuts his eyes and snores on a dirty bedroll.
Settlers bump hulls against his shoreline.

Colette Sensier

Graduation Wearing Salmon

Riddle

La Vanille Crocodile Farm, Mauritius

Graduation Wearing Salmon

Each particular space and time took you as far as the illusion
of Alexandria found in the fans or pages of brick, swept cold
around you, painting you in stone. Something you thought
                        you didn't know
hit you like a blue door swinging outwards over little whirls
                         like pebbles, damp mist...

For the first time you're taken into meaning, distant: that fur
                        jacket
you loved, catching the plane to Egypt, the race across the
                        quad one
afternoon. What will you find when you go back? Only the
                        dawn, pink and emerald
like salmon's gloves, open as pearl, carolling the only thing
                        left to say. Okay. Now run

over the grass they told you not to, the square with the
                        daisies
sticking up tall as buttercups, the buttercups like dandelions,
                        the dandelions
like hay. Remember always how every white striped pillar
                        fell towards the noon,
and reclined in the evening-time and morning, subtly as
                        glass; and a bird over our heads,

or perhaps the distant squeak of a swing, calling 'Who?', the bent
look in your face and the burn-marks on my shoe.
                        Remember the slow
roar, above, of aeroplanes, and colour a little god wherever
                        you find it. All I know
is a lock of hair moving through my eyeline like a curled
                        brown snake, and my thin skirt

on stone. Directly ahead a crane stands like a queen, glorious
in metal, flanked by traffic cones, deep blue. Someone could
                                         walk along
any of the parapets you see around you, his face the colour
                                         of the English sky
like a white-wall-papered room left to work itself through
                                         the daytime. Gravity,

both here, and now. Hold to it. Hold to the golden mean
they've shown you so well in the cutting of a poem or a face
into thirds, or in the triangular facet above those almost
                                         fading pillars,
standing in the unshaping sky proud as a burn, as your
                                         limitless options surround it.

Riddle

Who am I? I'm a long line of women picking pampas grass,
and in the same century and season, a vertical drop of
                                                            bankers.
Once, jumping like a flake of disused skin through scraped,

forsaking sky, and once, upturned as a hasty vomit-bucket
for the first visitors to Bolivia, who couldn't bear the altitude.
The fine leaves of cocaine, tobacco, coffee stain the teeth

below me as the owner's heads turn hot with calculation;
a strong blue buzz of numbers in the hard-racked brains, of
                                                            men
unable to add up, who still think that their feet will be the
                                                            first thing

to hit the ground. As they place me with unusual
                                        deliberation
on top of the old grey school tie which has failed them,
the same heat becomes a slow hum running over the
                                                            hairlines

of the women who took me in when I was hovering behind
ship doors uncertain of my future, an unsuitable refugee —
believing it to be the right, the fashionable thing to do.

In the market I waved in the arms of their own men,
on that stand between the witches' stall and the
                                            apothecary's.
I curved in the air and echoed magic words - Paris, London,
                                            modern,

bombshell, charm — scraped from the last barrel of
                                            capitalism.
What do you do with anything that's smaller than a man?
With water, flowers, new arrivals? As long as you don't cross
                                            them,

women are vain enough to take in anything.
(With something too big for any man - invasion, gold, the
                                                    ocean —
you must find the smallest, blankest spot — a window,
                                        crow's nest,

the crest of a white mountain. Tilt something over your eyes.
Distract yourself. Small sutures heal wounds.) Red leaves
scatter themselves onto the cold grey street by the pretzel
                                            wagon.

In Bolivia, the women continue to burn, to pick, or buy
the right things at the right time. Still working in their line,
they think of the next task – the need to slash open a llama's

round, black belly, and pull out her young — eyes closed,
                                        small
as your thumb — to bury as a talisman, good-as-any, in the
                                                hungry
earth beneath the floorboards of a fragile new dwelling.

La Vanille Crocodile Farm, Mauritius

We're sitting in the crocodile-farm restaurant
    eating crocodile steak off a long glass table,
    while the crocodiles circle hopefully below us,
    and I wonder how they kill them. Try a stun gun?
    Hope to get lucky with a bullet to the head?

No guilt in handbags, shoes, suitcases made
    from these crocodiles, when each one flayed
    drives down the value of her wild cousins' skin.
    Not unlike the siblings born in labs for organ
    harvesting, with anxious parents standing

behind glass in the Baby Unit, watching the precious
    marrow pump through living, dispensable bones.
    With false humility, you say that when you die,
    you want to be fed to the crocodiles. Someone
    else around the table declares her wish to be

cremated, and her ashes to be thrown then
    to the North wind, the fire stripping her of all
    unnecessary padding. Her way of saying to the vast
    savage green world, *I was only ever a visitor here,*
    I am a creature not of earth but air.

Richard O'Brien

The Day the Revolution Came

Honey in the Bible

Dry Land

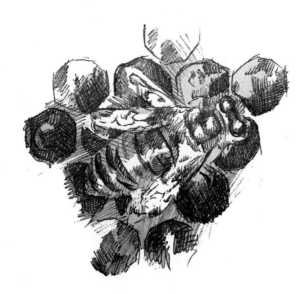

The Day the Revolution Came

The day the revolution came to Ruislip
there was fighting in the streets (but not too much.)
I myself greeted cars approaching on the ringroad
like a monkey in a safari park—off with their doors!
their loaded bikeracks!—while Terry from the sweetshop
broke into the petting zoo and sacrificed a lamb to Satan.

Anarchy in the supermarket aisles!
Some joker stacked the aubergines to ceiling height
and flew into them, screaming, on a zipwire.
I myself smeared my torso in banana pulp
and rolled around on the conveyor belt—
forwards! Always forwards!—
until the scanner went into meltdown.

Everybody in the church
upturned the pews and drew a tiger on the sexton's face.
He ran into the kitchen showroom, roaring.
O, misshapen chaos of well-seeming formica!
Fires in the bakeries! The collapse of well-intentioned signs!

And yes, the revolution *was* televised,
but reception's never been good on five, and besides
we were all out smashing an effigy of Eamon Holmes's face
with a rake. I myself got a few good kicks in,
then I stole a miniscooter and a petrol can
and made for the public library like van der Lubbe at the
                                                    Reichstag.

Ceremonially we burnt the entire Richard and Judy summer
                                                    book list.
We tore pages out of Frank O'Hara and pasted them
into the frontispieces of every book with 'Daughter' in the
                                                    title,

not including the ones we had already burnt.

I myself wore a hat that I would not normally wear,
and a woman with whom I had often played online chess
streaked down the High Street pursued by a wolf.
On closer inspection, the greengrocer
was inside the wolf. 'Take that, Bear Grylls!' he shouted
as he pulled her savagely to the pavement outside
                                                    Mothercare.

Loudhailers were employed and were ignored. I myself
showed a policeman a pornographic picture
on my mobile phone and secretly I think he liked it.
When they sent the helicopters we threw
prize fruit into the screaming blades.

John from Weightwatchers turned his back on the battle
to shove his face into a massive trifle, a chocolate one, with
                                        lots of sprinkles—
naughty John!—and Claire declared her love for me from
                                                    the roof
of Caffé Nero with nothing on her person but
a polystyrene cup in a small or medium size
and a smile tastier than caramel latte.

I tumbled upwards into her arms. Later, I heard
a seal was found in the outside swimming pool,
moaning its last as it writhed and died
in the scum and cigarette butts. Children laughed at the seal,
and named it Alastair Darling. I myself was not present,
but would have hurt it, though I might have felt bad
because it was really still a seal.

The Mayor had never seen the like! He frolicked briefly
with an underling in full view of his electorate
then sang a song of low repute and ran wailing, naked,

into the woods. Hours later his body was located
swinging from an elm and I myself would say
that's probably when the tension started to wind down.

Things are different now. We've seen each other's faces
closer than we'd like. I myself tasted the blood of an
                                                    alderman.
Mostly we stay inside these days. I open the curtains
and the doors on Sundays, a little, but not too much.

Honey in the Bible

When Samson broke the lion's jaws
its corpse was filled with honey.
He took a present for his father
from the consecrated temple of the bees.

Christ's Disciples gave him honey
when he rose to prove he had the lust
for sweetness of a living man,
and John the Baptist braved the desert with it.

Honey is prosperity; is commerce, sex
and medicine, the lipstick of a concubine
that Solomon transmutes into vermouth.
It could stop wars, gum up the wheels.

I know that you've seen war. If you've seen sweetness,
you don't show it. I'm on the back seat for a five-hour drive,
reading away the silence. I don't think you're noticing
the mountains either, by the way you're driving.

We've got honey in the basket, squeegee-bottle manna,
given as an offering to governors and kings;
and now to me. We're climbing; going on a picnic,
you and me, and honey. Abraham and Isaac.

Dry Land

Before the kiss things happened that were not
the kiss. These things included: crucifixions,
atom bombs, the rise and fall of Carthage, Trotsky's
death, the writing of the Periodic table, and inventions
such as television, microwaves and desk-lamps,
not to mention many minor incidents in which kisses
took place between princes, lexicographers, tramps,
various trades in the service industry, etc, etc—but this is
not relevant here. Before the kiss there was a long silence
of at least two seconds in which nothing happened at all
except for the clock's tick fighting its way through treacle
to emerge, sticky and bruised from its submarine violence
but finally, somehow retaining its grace, reaching the shore,
gasping for air like a lungfish.   It lasted a second or
                                                                    more.

Charlotte Geater

Lost in Broadcast

Soft

Boil

Lost In Broadcast

(after & i.m. — David Foster Wallace
and his *New York Times* article
about Roger Federer)

You raise an arm. The ball is just a...
gone. Like your hand on her shoulder when
you watched television together, ate pizza
and you felt like nothing more than linesmen

with half a lifetime lost to slow motion.
Love. When people you don't know watch you
repeatedly, know you, or on reflection
have been tricked by the deft clip of your shoe

on the grass centre-court, or *thank you, please
if it's no trouble,* the screen becomes, what?
Is it you? And your face in the rallies,
why is it frozen? The ball's like gunshot

caught doing its worst. You were so fast
and they can't know you from photographs.

Soft

describe my voice, she said.
use any word. make it a girly one.
I didn't answer so she kissed

her teeth at me, the glued-on diamond
glittered like a metal brace
caught full with saliva in the light
and she counted
one two three on her knuckles

tossed back her bronze hair, said
hardly any of these girly words
are about you and coughed—
my perfume like a hairball
   or a knife to her throat.

Boil

You broke the kettle. It is
your responsibility to buy
a new one. So you leave

work early and you're
still looking when it's late
night shopping and none

of them are right or cheap
enough. There's a catalogue
in argos and it's flashing

red toy cars at you, ruby
earrings that she would never
wear, a kettle that glows

when it's boiling, but nothing
that you want and the
tills have all broken so the assistants

are taking cash
at the door. Your black
nissan micra will not start.

You want to kiss the kettle
when you plug it in at midnight
after the long walk back

and it hums like the fridge
when you flick the button
on. The curtains are open.

Your garden is just
concrete that you cannot see.

Rees Arnott Davies

Amalfi

Saint-Malo

The Turk

Amalfi

The postcard says Amalfi,
nothing else.
Below the name sits coastline
roaring through the wordless

sky and seasick blue.
And there, again, Amalfi
in a different hand:
A M A L F I

Trying to set the scene,
I remember you climbing from rock to rock to
spit out on the flattened bay.
It seemed like that today,

with the postcard smudged through my
letterbox (smelt of morning rain),
climbing step to step back up into the flat
lay on my side and picture

us together there, signing in muted scenery,
swilling salt water under the initialled
tree, sweating palm to palm and trying to
forget the morning's rain, the afternoons of calm.

Saint-Malo

[archaeology for beginners]

when you come to low tide
and the clogged pockets
of footprint in the sand

churning cloud-light with the tinct of trod water,
mazed in their forgotten patterns
like the first words of the afternoon,

gather our things:
papers and bags, the towels and clothes.
Don't let us forget.

[blast]

the single voice of a Nightjar
breaks, multiplies in the top branches,
the quarter-moon sticks to the tarred windows,
the picture holds,

then
into the night fall a dozen fresh flashes
like the burning bind of magnesium,
opening the scene:

trees, plaster, pavement, air,
factored into the first thing.
But even amongst this wave of stone and flame
there still persists a solitary hair
floating
motionless like a single scratch on the lens.

[the museum]

as in a peat bog
the bodies stayed missing:
perfect, unused

and the city,
petrified,
-
stood like a museum piece.

In time, the wreckage would be reused,
buildings rebuilt from the same stones
in the same pattern,
as if by some conjuring trick.

But the memory, of bombs and blasts,
will still be stuck
behind the glass,
like in some old photograph.

The Turk

*'The story is told of an automaton chess player constructed in such a
way that it could play a winning game of chess, answering each move of
an opponent with a countermove. A puppet in Turkish attire and with a
hookah in its mouth sat before a chessboard placed on a large table.'*

[1]
He had been built on the cheap:
scrap leather, tarnished copper,
cogs from the guts of a grandfather clock
and the full four strings of a viola.
Around him the garb of a sorcerer.

[2]
'A match for any challenger,
this, the Turk, will clock
your moves before they're made.
Who among you dares to face
the hand that's toppled kings
and captured queens?'

[3]
There were rumours,
there were diagrams and theories,
but who could claim to know the workings of the Turk?

Who knew more, even, than the washer-woman
said to have heard the spirit trapped within, swearing?

[4]
In the Hall of Mirrors
the only moving thing
was the hand of the Turk
and its reflection.

[5]
and the prisons were emptied
and the palaces were emptied
and the Turk called checkmate.

[6]
history is black and white
and ends in the guillotine for some.
His hand ranged over the pieces

[7]
In Vienna, London, Potsdam
the story was the same—
princes terror-struck,
streetlamps unlit,
minds unravelled by a mere bagatelle.

[8]
She swore she'd seen
inside the Turk,
and inside the Turk
she'd seen a mirror.

[9]
In the palaces of Old Europe
he'd sung on cue, like clockwork,
checking Benjamin Franklin,
frustrating Napoleon Bonaparte,
sparkling.

Now in Philadelphia,
a hunchback slumped
a beat behind the New World
ghosting moves, moth-eaten
rusting, rotting, killing time.

[10]
Flames filled the museum windows
with grave sunlight,

and through the flaking applause,
the Turk's last word
(a spectre of the first) burst forth:
checkmate

Annie Katchinska

Massachusetts

Panic Attack

Massachusetts

By its ghost towns of toffee and dust
I'm sorely tempted—the shutters crumpling
in on themselves like cream.

The spices from the pink hotels just long to be licked.
I watch them melt, scrape
the windows with my peppery tongue;

crawl into their evergreen palaces
and great libraries, snap icicle spines;
I steal their yellowing gardens

petal by petal. The dead woman's dress
will soon be a ragged eyelash because of me.
I'll slurp the children's milk bottles dry

and gouge out the beaks of ravens and use
my teeth and claws to mangle presidents' eyes.
Anyone would, in a town where all day

the sky's paint sticks to your bones;
where the streets turn golder and golder, I lick
cake-crumbs of rust from their doors.

Panic Attack

"Here we go" the wiry woman says
opening the door to the insect circus—
this is the place where beetles tremble in autumn
whirring round on sugary nickel hoops

Girls bare furry teeth
and wind up ladybirds on tightropes for me,
a bluebottle towers by a trapdoor, and hums
In a corner marked CLOWNS
they're feeding a fat mouth candifloss
There's a glow-worm in a box
There are fleas of glitter stuck round a mirror
where you can see my hands, and a dirty flying ant
battling my breath's
clumsy cartwheels

I stagger to the trapdoor
and its delicate sign
Please touch the bluebottle gently

Rowena Knight

Charon's Passengers

At Sea

Angel Beach

Charon's Passengers

They cling to their myths: the boat with room for only one,
plus me, and space left over for their tragedy. To tell their
tale
as old Charon thrusts his pole into the water
surely and smoothly, in a darkness which is only a distant
cousin
to our night. To know he is listening,
though he keeps his moon-white eyes on the river,
makes no sound but the slap and shift
of his palms on the pole. Do they have any idea
how inefficient it would be to take souls across that way?
Each seems to think they are the only one to die today,
sees their name as the hub of my day's work—
and this is work to me. I don't ask for names,
only cash. Remain professional. What do they expect?
My ferry takes five thousand, and names won't buy bread.
They come to my shore, mouths full of their tales,
but fall quiet when given their room key
and introductory pamphlet, and say no word
to the cracked plastic chairs, the scent of disinfectant
veiling vomit. Most ignore the new pool and gymnasium,
choose instead to spend the trip watching the river
and chewing overpriced candy bars from the gift shop.
Replaying their deaths in their heads, I suppose,
or wondering if it's possible to get bumped up to first class.
Last month I had so many ask
that I added a new line to the introductory pamphlet:
ALL ROOMS OF SIMILAR STANDARD. PASSENGERS
MAY NOTE,
THERE IS NO FIRST CLASS IN DEATH.

At Sea

A boy in one hand and a drink in the other
and I know I should be watching the boy,
watching his hands,
checking they're anchored at my waist,
checking his eyes are full of me, not horizon
but all I'm thinking is how small my hands are,
and is it just me or is this drink getting bigger,
am I holding it or is it holding me. I had it.
I had my fingers wrapped round it, I was counting the ticks
of the clock, I was one sip a minute then I tripped
on the hour hand and found myself in the glass,
fumbling in foam and the boy

I should be watching the boy, I know that—
they told me when his sails are full
he's off and you can't signal to him, he's off following a light
flashing from a pretty girl not me
in an ocean of shoulders and pint glasses. But then
if he's anchored am I stuck in this pub,
is he pulling me down, am I stuck in one place
with him and his hands. So much bigger than mine hands
are all I can think of, I swear my fingernails are shrinking
like sails on the horizon. And the sun's going down
and he's looking at me and I drank too much,
I swam too far out but

how can I escape an ocean when I can't remember
the last time my hands were free, or how many nights
it's been since I clutched only at cool sheets,
and pressed only the lips of a pillow to my cheek

Angel Beach

He kissed my eyes awake when I was thirteen.
Epiphany hot and sweet as December,
sand light as prayers
stuck to feet, navel, hair.
The sky opened like an eye,
left me dizzy. We pocketed shells
for offerings, had our coke communion.
The beach sang with us,
the bach like an untuned guitar
full of praise. Hands warm and heavy
as sun on my back
as we collected each other's tears.
Enough salt water to fill a horizon with faith,
to swim in its green.
We were sure the feathers that spined our feet
were left by angels,
that even the ringing song of frogs
was a repetition of his name.

Note: "bach" is a New Zealand term for "holiday home".

Emily Middleton

Breakfast with the Gods

Poppy Harvesting

The Faces

Breakfast with the Gods

Northwest Tuscany: a small fishing town.
I left my comrades behind, their bodies still bent
like broken bayonets under the creases
of the army-issue blanket.

Seeing the rock in that picture...
the sixty-year gulf between now and that morning—
the other wars (you won't remember), the courtship
and frugal plainclothes wedding, the firm

and its progression, peak, and crash
in the recession, the retirement
to this 'castle'...blah de blah blah...
all of it shrinks to an inch, an mp3 file—

now I can reach out and touch the rock
bleeding its guts of moss-slime;
the semi-circle of sun breaking the horizon
and mixing new shades with the sea's waves.

I stand without slipping, bend my knees
and am gone in the time a fruit-fly is born,
mates then dies; the earth revolves once
while I am suspended (as a fly in a spider's plate)

in Apollo's molten golden slipstream,
then the seawater, sprinting, encases my brain,
precise as a Roman battle formation.
My head fills with holes like coral.

Salt coats my throat and eyeballs;
the lifecycles of stars speeded-up in sapphire
pop before my eyes like children's balloons—
twisting, I violate Neptune without permission.

My euphoric march back to the barracks:
I am Jupiter striding along the cobbled streets,
weaving between fishmongers and florists, tracing the path
of emperors, dripping with victory, with sea and sweat.

Poppy Harvesting

When I was younger, I watched through the window:
the burly workers with their arms threaded with bulging bulbs,
hacking and scything, slaughtering flowers by the thousands.

When I was older, I watched from the doorway:
half-naked men, three dozen Adonises burned gold by the
sun,
baskets of poppies strapped to their backs, bent double

under their iron weight, beads of sweat streaming like smoke
from a second-hand shell. From the yard, I waved goodbye
as their baskets turned to muskets; their labourers' shirts

to pressed green uniforms boasting buttons of silver.
Then, the pastures were empty; the poppies left to anarchy.
We watched the field grow bloodier,

stalk torsos choking and clotting until it regressed
to an unchallenged block of blinding, mesmerising colour.
Finally, we began to harvest

ourselves: slowly at first, with strawberry boxes,
then wheelbarrows meant for farm work.
We were lauded in the papers;

abandoned our kitchens and hearths
to live under the real heat, relishing the aeroplanes' breeze
on our faces. But soon enough the old men—

mud and sweat striped tigers—returned to the poppy field,
dreaming of scarlet arteries and ventricles.
We returned to our homes, and watched through the pane

as the baskets were filled right up to the scalp,
bursting with poppy heads, blood-red and dead,
whilst our stews burned and blackened on the stove.

The Faces

After five thousand years,
we've found the faces.

Two of them, like bugs in amber,
wide-eyed with dying smiles.

The crowd starts the chant
as the shaman raises his knife

and bellows, stone-throated,
like a mountain god:

After five thousand years,
we've found the faces.

He begins to peel
and the skin falls away,

flaking fast like drying clay;
and he reaches inwards,

grasps the memories,
onyx-coloured, congealing

like computer wires
or Medusa's snakes.

After five thousand years
we've found the faces.

Antony Hurley

Exile

The Morning Garden

An August Evening with W.B. Yeats

Exile

Under the London lites and leaves
That scope forgotten parks,
In this desert of parallel streets
Nothing can truly connect

Yesterday, two hands could find each other and
Live for a day in all corners;
Peace Pagodas, Williams Hills, Fulham Broadway, Tedworth
square—
They had it all

Tonight this place will not accommodate us,
Show me the long way home:
The 23:47 from Charing Cross,
Go through tube gates, up rolling escalators,
Toss change to the beggar; pass the melodica man
I'm on my way now, back home,
To this, my exile's end.

The Morning Garden

A sorry vole peels the cat's ears and a stray
Dog shifts the bins
Those who sleep are locked in folded graves,
They do not stir; even the birds are not awake

Paths branch from the copper road, lined with ginger
Shrubs and leafy shrouds
Roots creep under moistened earth, oblivious to
Snoring owners, no hopers walking in a dream

Benches stand alone; stiff as stolen church pews,
Frozen in rows, they wait for morning mass

Morning asks no question, it creeks in fountains,
Beats in drains, shivers puddles and skates in icy lanes,

It rises with the dawn, then is stolen by the sun in the
                                        second
Between an eyelid opened and the realization
That day's begun.

An August Evening with
W.B. Yeats

Evening sank into a wash of watercolour blue,
I took your hand and followed you

Between the splinters of marble and old stones,
Under the restless willows

We sat on the cannons in Tite Street;
She told me the tragedies of a man who she saw
Slumped on a wall outside Parson's Green, dying unseen

Past the graves,
Through the daffodils and lily waves

I took your hand and followed you.

The poets

Rees Arnott-Davies is studying English Language and
Literature at St John's College, Oxford. He was a runner-up
in the Tower Poetry competition 2007.

John Clegg lives in Cambridge/Manchester, and intends
to start a PhD at the University of Durham in 2009. He
has recently completed an MA on 'Vermin in Twentieth-
Century Poetry'. A chapbook should be published by tall-
lighthouse early in 2010.

Charlotte Geater was at Northgate High School in Ipswich
until 2008. She was a Tower Poetry prizewinner in 2006
and 2008 and is now reading English at St Edmund Hall,
Oxford. She was a Foyle Young Poet winner in 2005, 2006
and 2007.

Antony Hurley studied at Tonbridge School, Kent. After
travelling extensively in South America he is enjoying the
comforts of home before reading English Literature at
Leeds University.

Annie Katchinska won 2nd prize in the Tower Poetry
competition 2007 and studied at St Dunstan's College
before Cambridge where she is reading Classics
at Pembroke. She is going to be published in the
forthcoming anthology "Voice Recognition: 21 Poets for the
21st-Century" (Bloodaxe Books)

Rowena Knight is in her second year at Durham University
studying History and Classics. She was a commended
Foyle Poet in 2006 and has been published on the
Pomegranate ezine, Forced Rhubarb and Rising magazines
and in the anthology for the Great Writing website. Her
favourite things include Greek tragedy, Tegan and Sara,
green spaces and spelling, though she has yet to discover
a way to combine all four successfully.

Ailie MacDonald has just completed a degree in English Literature & Creative Writing at the University of Warwick, and is spending the summer working with the National Trust for Scotland. She has previously been published in Agenda Poetry magazine as one of the chosen Broadsheet young poets.

Emily Middleton won 1st prize in the 2008 Tower Poetry competition and studied at Kings School, Manchester before reading English at Wadham College, Oxford.

Richard O'Brien was a runner-up in the 2008 Tower Poetry competition. He studied at Bourne Grammar School, before reading English and French at Brasenose College, Oxford. His first pamphlet comes out from tall-lighthouse in September 2009.

Colette Sensier won 1st prize in the 2007 Tower Poetry competition and took part in the 2007 and 2008 Summer Schools. She is now at Cambridge studying English and has also been a winner of the Foyle's and Peterloo prizes and has been published in the Rialto, Monkey Kettle and the Mays anthology.